IN RANGE

RODRIGO TOSCANO

IN RANGE

Counterpath
Denver
2019

Counterpath
Denver, Colorado
www.counterpathpress.org

ISBN 978-1-93-399673-8

Library of Congress Cataloging in Publication Data
is available from the Library of Congress.

For Stanlyn Brevé

STORAGE

Commit to being
With whole body and mind
The sages suggest

From there flows not truth
But the possibility of truth
If you step up

It's possibility of truth pursued
That makes for meaning
Shared or not shared

In the case of shared
One attends to responses
From others comes definition

In the case of unshared
It's stored, occulted from view
Till it dies, quietly

At any rate
Deaths, silent or loud
Is what's in store

So tidying up the store front
Is a welcomed task
And welcomed sight for the curious

WEEDING

I mean, how much weeding can one do?
Over and over, they return
Tenacious, lustful, proliferous

And what qualities befit weeding?
Determination, doggedness, futility
Over and over I return

If weeds and I engage fully
The score spread is close to zero
This is boredom defined O Reader

But before this game's ended
I want to say this—and *mean* it
You might take to weeding

To properly do weeding
Plants must be cherished
Better yet, if planted by you

Which brings up *planting*
Which in turn summons *soiling*
Which calls out to *crafty hands*

And now, we're set up quite nicely
Some dickhead can suggest
Weeding is like poem making

And that hails, no, howls
To boredom, a new height
Its qualities: droop, nod, doze

But stick around a bit
We don't *have to* poemize nor weed
How about a quick stroll around the garden?

BRICK SEALANT

And I immediately imagined the steps' undoing
A pile of refuse, after renovation, 100 years from now

A lonely clump of bricks, alter to nothingness, submerged in
    water 200 years from now
And, most frightful, nobody doting on that task, or steps, their
    destiny

DAMN MULCH

Who the fuck knows
How they float into the pool
Ceaselessly splashing, swaying the day away

Some pieces take in sun at the surface
Others submarine in the middle depths
Yet others, play dead, stuck to the bottom

I survey the entire scene
Or the entire scene is revealed to me
Or a revelation harkens itself to itself

Whichever, soon the beast is unleashed
A simple press of a red button
And the vacuum on the pole begins to growl

Are y'all excited yet?
Can I get *grr grr?*
CAN I GET A GRR GRR?

Twenty minutes later
Satisfaction comes over me
I *can* get some, I *can* get some

The front shield is unsnapped
The mesh filter is removed
Damn mulch is tossed over the fence

I survey the entire scene
Or the entire scene is revealed to me
Or the revelation harkens itself to itself

While a merry six or so
Damn mulches
Dance their way to the pool

CAULKING

That's with an 'a' 'u' 'l'—caulking
Ever caulked any of y'all—skillfully?
Caulking cracks, you know

Ever any all y'all filled a hole
Squeeze a caulk tube
Few last gobs to spread, pack?

How many all y'all handled a cualking gun?
Some all y'all too trigger happy?
Anybody in here nicknamed trigger, froggy, bobo?

With an 'a' 'u' 'l'—I say to the clerk—caulk—where do you keep it?
With an 'a' 'u' 'l'—aisle 22
With an 'o' 'm' 'g' —let's keep 'o' 'c' 'k'—at bay

WRONG SOAP

Filled all pump bottles
With the wrong liquid
Foam won't come out

And all of humanity now
Wants to know what
Happens when they're pumped

Spoiler alert 1: nothing
Spoiler alert 2: nothing
Spoiler alert 3: nothing

WELL WISHERS

"Thank you, may god bless you"
Panhandler says to atheist
How might atheist deal with that?

Atheist might bear down on "thank you"
Brushing off the "may god" etc.
He's well practiced in that

Atheist might also ponder afterwards
How can a mere mortal front for a deity?
And what *approximately* does "may" mean?

Atheist might also inquire on the spot
What *kind* of blessing?
Answer given: "what god wills"

Atheist might translate that as
"Who the hell knows, man", or
"You shouldn't be asking that, man"

Atheist might imagine a different order
"May good fortune come upon you"
As coins drop into an open hand

But then the quandary "may"
Ceases the matter in its grip
Squeezing the life out of the exchange

Atheist then might resign himself to custom
The order of Who blesses Whom and Why
And on behalf of Whom

Atheist might at a different moment altogether surmise
What if both atheism *and* theism don't actually matter
Hm. May it be so

FUMIGATION DAY

Today's the day I said I'd do it
How to say that in French and German
Never mind, today's the day

What's the very first thing to do?
Get out of the tub, dry off
What's the next thing

Ok, in the *midst* of fumigating
What's important, what's not so important
And how do you say that in French and German?

When the task is completed
How much pride is to be taken
In proportion to humility unto the next task?

But I've told myself to stop these calculations
Mais je me suis dit d'arrêter ces calculs
Aber ich habe mir gesagt, diese Berechnungen zu stoppen

PANTS

How do I look in these pants?
How do you look in those pants?
Do I *wanna* wear pants?

Wait. Do you *want* to wear pants?
Do we want to wear underwear
Under or *over* our pants?

Well, *that* trend won't last long
Some might get off on it, yes
Today, yes, when else?

SLINGSHOT

But when I saw the delivery van from Aaron's
Bopping along my pot-holed street
I felt a surge of gentleness

That somebody put some amount of heart
Into that business that sells sofas and mattresses
Somebody imagined that crummy logo

More than that I thought
People have to sit, lay down, lounge too
And Aaron's is here to help with that

But I tried my darnest to shatter that back store lamp
That blinding beam that showers our bedroom at night
Eight direct hits and nothing

Not two weeks ago, I pinged the previous lamp to bits
But this new one's made out of a special plastic
And honestly, I'm quite relieved by that

LAWN

The state of my front lawn
Concerns me
And *that* concerns me

Still though, action
Is what lies ahead
Though, not really

What's here now
Are syllables
One by one by one

So, three levels of concern
A triple decker
To bite into, chew

Meanwhile, the lawn
As the lawn
Played by the lawn

And nitrogen solution
An action stunt bit player
Ready in the wings

Me, I'm chewing syllables
Not counting this time
But feeling them—you feel me?

SQUEAKY DOOR

Too friggin squeaky
For my taste

Desired: a quiet entrance
Desired: a quiet exit

Great thing about grease
It eases passage

People the world over
Seek greases of all kinds

Listen closely to random chatter
Folks sick of squeaking and screeching

Desired: a smooth solo
Desired: a smooth ensemble

Ok, sometimes creaking and rasping
Ok, sometimes even a hard jam

And what's the point of poetry
If ain't slick

PILL TRAY

Repetitive, fatiguing, defeating
But here it is
Again and again

Sunday, Monday, Tuesday
Wednesday, Thursday, Friday
Saturday—*never* forgo Saturday

Clumps o' pills in waiting
Same set, same time
When empty, refill all seven slots

How'd life get this calculated?
Or was it there all along
Everything in parcels, doses

How may days in a row completed?
How many days skipped?
And what the hell were in those trays anyway?

SEEDS

I mean, just one tree
I've been scoping
Must've shed a million

And *zero* will sprout
Landing on pavement, or
Resting on rooftops

Such a show too
Shit splattering everything
Piling up, clump on clump

Some in this town battle it
Blowing it hither and thither
Rearranging the mess

Each single seed's fate
All but foretold
To dust, finer and finer

The "battle" thus ends
Some claiming victory
Gathering, mound on mound

MEDITATIO SCRIBENDI

A half baked Robert Frost
Primed by two shots of
Everette Maddox, *alas*

HOSES

The math of entanglement
Cylindricals entwined complexity
Hard jacks the frontal cortex

The *practice* of disentanglement
Matter's limits + desired outcome
Hard jacks the temporal lobe

"Gotta keep these two hoses separate
Can't be pretzeling up"
Hard jacks the medulla oblongata

C-rings along a fence
Threading one hose through—isolate
Hard jacks the occipital lobe

All the brain's parts are entangled
All brains—are entangled
Thy name is: Jacko Homo

PALM FRONDS

When the frost hit us
When the frost hit us
Ok, let me tell this

When the frost hit us
Frying the palm fronds
Frying me—actually

Right, we, or rather, I
Didn't know what to do
I knew what to do!

OK, you tell it
I stood, fried, day and night
Yes, steadfastly, you stood

I was stressed out for you
Yeah? I never knew that
I still don't know that

I know, that too, stresses
Though I accept it
And found a remedy

And you found a remedy
In a state of acceptance
Of my sentience?

Yeah, went to Home Depot
Got me a pole saw
To trim you down

And trimmed me down you did
To an extreme!
I'm left baked and bare

Oh come on now
Most of you—is your roots
That's true—true as frost

Very well said that
Though you haven't, really
Nor have you, bud, for reals

POOL DECK REVERIE

About some thirty years ago
A poet some twenty years my senior
Fumed about some reading ten years before

He said, "it went on *and on*
One stanza for tanning dick, *right side*
One stanza for tanning dick, *left side*"

Like that, he retold it
Imparting disgust as moral injunction
How unredeemable the event was

Needless to say, this elder
Deemed himself a revolutionary
And this youngin aspired to such

No revolution came
Instead, a ceaseless flopping
Now right, now left; now left, now right

And the mystery of that terrible poem
The Tanner, let's just say
Apparently lives on

Let One Hundred Golden Asses Bloom!
Right here! Right now!
Or, whenever's, fine

ADHESIVE

Gorilla Glue
(I hope I don't need permission for that)
Might adhere this darn speaker

If I can just get up that high
Without risking a fall
I'll give it a go

But an old sensation seizes me
Like I need to ask permission
To even *ask* permission

That, and the cracked out Gorilla
Which sought *no* permission
Inching me onwards

LITTLE FENCE

Little Fence #1
Was a rusty, crooked
Barely standing tangle of wire

Day by day, I built up
A feigned animus for it
Plotting its downfall

The hour finally came
When I hired the gator hunter
To build little Fence #2

Shiny, erect, newly sprung
An even mesh of wire
Feigning delight in my doting

I suspect #1 is
At the bottom of this
Interposed as #2

Or in a truly freaky twist
It might can be #3
Plotting a downfall

Free floating gator
Tangled cloud overhead
Poppin a top at noon

TOOLS

How many damn tools
Can a man buy
Week after week

You'd think a sort of ark
Was being stuffed to the brim
With crap like this

The glorious result will be
Not half a half person
Will be able to wedge in

Bon voyage noble ark!
May eternal preparedness
Find you a mountain top

When a sun beam burns through
When the receipts twitter and flutter
May the tools tool around—*free*

NEXT TASK

OK, *this* one
Takes the cake
From the get go

What *possibly*
Can this achieve
This *puttering*

You know what I mean?
A circular motion
As linear triumph

This one—*what*
Is for the fates?
Or rattled nerves?

Or *neither*
And *less* than neither
A blank hole

A hole to fit into
Me, the size of me
Filling out the fabric, cosmic

DOFFING GLOVES

Alright, yeah, one accepts being
For a good stretch of time
Until the quandary turns stale

Until that time though
Clear the mulch two inches
And add a 4-inch retainer wall

Maybe it's about donning gloves
Or scraping piece by piece
Maybe it's about *doffing* gloves

Unlike this here though
It's not about recognition
Or fucking wait a second

They think he's a border poet
They think he's Mr. Labor
They think he's *experimental*

Wrong, wrong, *wrong*
Right, no yeah, right
When it storms, hope my levees hold

FEED A STRAY

First thing
That paper plate
So sad, oof

Wants to flap
Or flop
Something

Second thing
Tuna mound is
Collapsing

Wants to slip
Or slide
Something

Third thing
Cat stays away
Thirty yards

Wants to come
Or scram
Something

TATTERS

Easiest thing to do is
Actually *not* the easiest
To give in, fully

A perilous moment
Of no promises
To unfold

The clock of time
Is the body
As far as words go

But there's more
The body's *in* society
And society's *in* hyperspace

It's hard to conceive
Hyperspace expanding
Leaving all in tatters

Poems try to forestall it
The body's probably in on it
Society's oblivious to it

MEDITATIO SCRIBENDI II

Or maybe George Herbert
Dry humping Nicanor Parra's
Wily ghost (whoa)

STARS AND STREET LAMPS

About to dis the stars
Ridic how distant
Buffoonish tease

And now post-navigational
And divvied up by type
The whole show sucks

Must there be a new show?
If the street lamps went out
Would the sky strike us with wisdom?

If not, can we each decide
If the show sucks
Or if it's just intermission?

If so, would everyone
Speak the same wisdom
Or remain as street lamps, occultive?

MONKEY GRASS

These bushy clumps
Aren't strictly grass
Much less monkey-like

Yet it pleases the mouth
And thus the ears
To hear it

The visuals too, please
Come to think of it
Froofed up monkey-like

I mean to say, monkeys
Like monkeys, and
Not so strictly

And it pleases the heart
To share the words
Somewhat strictly

GREEN STICK

Says on the label
That in California
This is toxic shit

Not so in Louisiana
Just one more condiment
In deathbed gumbo

But enough morbosity
The stick's designed purpose
Now beckons forthrightly

When these no-name plants
Droop too low 'for comfort'
(Who's comfort—an open debate)

Then stick one up *in* there
Rope up discomfort
For the time being, stand tall

OBJECTS

Objects *object*
To objectification
Subjectively

Subjects *subject*
Subjectification
Objectively

Monkey brains
Are at cross-purposes
Eating monkey grass

CONTENDERS

Rumors of remedies
For tasks big and small

Tales of varmints
Appearing and disappearing

Reports of real estate fluctuations
Laments, celebrations, befuddlement

Familial planning, stresses, unspooling
Dice rolls for hope

What else, encircling?
Vying to crush the center

Outlines of future pleasures
In avoidance of present pain

Of course, the T-Man
Vortex über alles

Add: glimpses of free will
Willed by wills unknown

Finally, bodily pricks and pranks
Pinching you back to wakeful sleep

GROCERY BAG

Eastwardly sailing
Painless, carefree

Momentarily caught up
Billowing, fluttering

Now ripping free
A big hole in it

Flattening, a bit listless
A slow drag

Into a crevice, clumping
Dirt packing it down

There is no reversing time
While the illusion of forward, works

MEDITATIO SCRIBENDI III

Two tiny sprinkles of
Emily Dickenson into
Li Po's moon-lit lake (mwah)

FENCES

How—*in the world*
Were thirteen poems
Written in one shot?

Fences everywhere
At the same hour
Lost their power

Could end it like that
This poem, for sure
And still might

But that's a fence
To say that
Fences being fuckers

But aside from fences & fuckers
Gathered here
Fence repair work's—round the bend

GAS POWERED BLOWER

All that went into it
Its separate components
The human work involved

How the thing works
Each and every time
As designed to

All of those folks assembled
Standing in a ring
Two hundred? Several thousand?

I wanna see them all
Right now, as they are
As I prime the starter ten times

The roar and howl is a chorus
With me at the center
Purpose being multifold and fluid

CLOVER

A thorough raking and turning of the dirt
A blanket of toxins sprayed thick
A half ton of granite rock spread out

You're going to be ok little clover
King, for now, you've sprouted
I know, this poem's been writ *a million times*

MOLDISIANA

Mold here, mold there
Impossible really
To fit into words

Let's try though
Mmmolding
Mmmooolllding

Nice try, but
No go
Things just, you know

'Moldisiana'
Not bad, eh?
Think it prize worthy?

SPELLS

Pool valves cast a spell on the distribution hub
Hub cast one on the water pump

Pump cast one on the power panel
Panel cast one on the breaker box

Box cast one on the electric meter
Meter cast one on the checking account

Account cast a doozy on the
Where does one get a fuckin' hand grenade? seriously!

PEPPERS

Private jet overhead
Neighbors dodging deportation
Just down the street—gunfire

Tankards of tourists
From all over—wowed
Peppers! next act—wait

2.5 mil mansion quarter mile away
90K ramshackle hut two blocks down
Peppers! next act—wait

Dude just outta jail
Across the street
Dude behind, back in

Tankards of tourists
From all over—wowed
Peppers! next act—wait

Jets—come and gone
Household here's—hangin' in
Outside Mr. Unmedicated—barking

Half dozen middling types
Folks with gardens—barking
Truth is, no peppers this year, sorry

CRACKS

Tension settling
In that corner
Makes for a crack

Houses' equilibrium
Never quite right
Same for the body

While we're at it
Pressurizing the mind
Same play of forces

You want some serenity
While chasing out boredom
But chasing's pressurizing

And thus a crack occurs
Known to you or not
Others *might* notice it

I ought not let it bug
But do, a tad
Having fixed the shit *four times*

TRASH DAY

Is it Monday?
Or Tuesday?
Then Thursday, right?

How does this
Not sink in
I hear the truck

Can't pop out
Naked and wet
There goes the truck

Yeah, yeah
Some moral's brewing
A universalism?

Haul it out Wednesday night
For now, dream landfills
Sinking and sinking

COCKRAGO FUCKSCANO

Buried in my backyard
I found a polyurethane idol
From a people centuries past

The house that was here before
Was transported on a barge
To Yuma, Arizona

When the flashflood hit
I deployed my car's wings
And flew to Yuma, California

"All 120 city pumps were working
On August 5, 2017"
My legal name is: Fuckrago Cockscano

MOON AGAIN

Same beef of old
So close, so far
Same for any "view"

Can't touch it
Can't smell it
Can't nothing to it

There it goes
Over the oak
Under the palm

No point to say
It's an exhibitionist, or
It's a voyeur

The glow just glows
Alright, ok, "the tides"
And cyclones and hollerin'

Am I *done* with views?
Or hankerin' for one
Bathed in the glow, touched

PASTORAL

Not four inches underground
It's total silence
How much above—500 hundred feet?

Depends on the city
Depends on the activity
Depends on the audio ability

But there's select pockets
At least in this city
How about your city?

Where litter yourself
For a quicky quick
Away from obelisks and costuming

AVANT-GARDE HEMLOCK

Now with a title like that
The shit's sure to fly

I was about to go on stage
In a swamp east of the city

Let's try that again:
On stage—in a swamp—east

Shit! Take cover!
Duck on outta here

OK, I'm back now—in a tossed tire
Somewhere in the city—in a swamp

Nah, bud, wouldn't call it a stage really
Nor you my target audience

LAWN MOWER

Strange trail of cut grass
Lawn chair propped up next to fence
Mower tarp flapping, empty

Now the spikes go up
Now the cameras are firing up
No, not getting a gun

This is trying
This is too routine
This requires *effective* procedures

Hope the mower's broke
Wish the re-sale owner the best?
No, not getting a gun

Now the lawn's poppin' up
Big party around the corner
This requires *effective* procedures

Strange trail of cut grass
Strange bag of feelings
And still—no, but thanks

SUN AGAIN

Seriously, friend or foe?
Silly to slobber over it
Inadvisable to block it out

Not a word can be said about sun
Not a word outside its sway
Showing a way

There's really nothing here
But sun—in sun mode
Confabulating a tale:

"I wasn't appointed
And I don't appoint
Don't be disappointed

I'm everyone's artist
I'm the art that's never been
Showtime's at 6:00 a.m. today

I'll be neither 'nurturing'
Nor 'killing' anything
Contrast's a delusion, yours"

Seriously, cool or *not* cool
The sun—in sun-mode
Silly to simmer on it too long

BRIGHT BLUE STAR

Tell you what's on *fire*
The notion of cold space

I *was* looking at it like that
From twinkle to pulsing eye

Took it about 15 million years
To reach me as I am

Coldest space between us
Firin' up the night

It *is* on the lookout for us
In a manner of speaking

Don't go negative, folks
Don't spout about "the collapse of time"

Focus—pocus—stay on point
There *is* an *inner out*

WINDOW WASHING

Fuck man, no way
Streaks, squiggles, blurs
Impossible to avoid

What's the *point* of this?
Signaling class mobility
As clear visibility?

Why not a smeary glob
To squint through
Exactly as this is

Lights out, lights on
Folks rising, folks falling
At the mercy of legacy and policy

Get cher squeegee on!
Work on the shit, man
Don't matter no how

The point's—coming to town
It's coming to town, soon
The town's—coming—to a point

TRUSTY PENCIL

You never fail me
Unlike an ink pen
When pressed to paper

I love re-tapering you
In twisting motion
Corkscrewed shavings falling

What will you tell me today?
I'm eager to listen
Almost too eager

Another coast eroding?
Another far-right victory
Another inner-left implosion?

Wait, you say leave it be?
Wait, you say brush it off?
Wait, you say kick it away?

But all these *actions*
Bind trouble to trouble
In one globular mass

There, the choristers commence
Poets for trusty messes
Poets for—this, that—the other

Time for re-tapering
Corkscrewed shavings falling
To stay in range

THE SEARCH

Was it Hume, or who
When playing billiards
Bolted—of a sudden

Something about that
He "realized" that
There's no world outside

Let's go find Hume
Maybe at the *Saturn Bar*
Or buzzing into *Pal's*

Where *is* Hume?
Let's see, look
Super carefully

Hey, try not to look like
You swallowed the outside
In one single schlook

DECK CHAIRS

Building all eight's gonna take what
Three hours or so?
By the numbers, we live

It takes a *long* long time
To face one's own distortions
Clearing the slate's a bitch

But in between *pure* work is *real* work
And best if self assigned
Not counting the minutes and hours

These chairs are crooked!
And two bolts are missing!
How in the world can this be?

Ten hours on assembly line *assigned*
One hour for eighteen verses *assigned*
WHO'S SLATES? OUR SLATES!

Gotta make due for now
Returning them's just as costly
Time to get on this

Not minding the minutes
Somewhat counting the days
Trying not to count the years

MEDITATIO SCRIBENDI IV

On a skiff, the Nicolás Guillén
Struggling up river with John Donne
Gotta unload the cargo (me too)

STRING LIGHTS

Super enjoyable!
Hours of enjoyment!
Enjoy, enjoy

Ah, string lights!
All strung up
One, one, one

Wait—again
One, one, *one*
One, one ... one

Super!
Super strung
All at once

Lit, lit, lit
Ooh, so
So—Lit

MR. OKRA

For those from outta town
Who never heard, saw
He was the midday sun's delight

Cruised around in a beat up truck
With wooden shelves
Stocked with vegetables

Up and down the streets
In *slooow* mow
Winding through the Marigny

And on a loud speaker
On *that* loud speaker
In a forever time now

"Aaaaaai've got OH-*kra*
I've got peeeeeez and po-tayyy-*toes*
I've gaaaaht—*onions*"

That was ages ago, folks
Like, two weeks ago
In the Age of Mr. Okra

SECURITY CAMS

Left/right corridors monitored
Front flanks covered
Back area secured

There, all three perimeters
Viewed continuously
By feats of engineering

Things that can't be easily tracked
Sudden puffs of malevolent smoke
Meandering miasmas of filth

What kind of equipment
Can be deployed for vying ideologies
Gliding in through walls and floors?

Course I don't believe in specters
Consumer solutions to
Primate Clusterfucks

DUMAINE AT BROAD GALLERY

"We wanna see some art"
But the moment you say 'we'
It's full on faux-realism

Upside down basketball hoop
Sporting a ripped t-shirt
Hammered to a tilted pole

"I wanna see some art"
But can art exist for "I"?
In' that faux realism too?

Pink wig no. 8 spread out
Like road kill, quit still
Follicles glittering the lawn

"Art wants to be seen"
Imperial faux-realism!
Kicked to the curb

Five tall boy Dixie cans clanking
Escorted by ten Po' Boy wrappers
Over four hunkerin' potholes

The *pièce de résistance?*
Violet RAV4 bouncing in
Crawls to a stop—door pops open!

VELCRO

Home security sign keeps tipping
Any breeze knocks it over
Post won't go any deeper

Soluzione (let's speak Italian!)
One square Velcro on the house
One square Velcro on the sign

Feel like Cesar conquering Gaul
Is a shaky simile
Given the thousands that *did*

Brings up another *do*
The old man planting a tree thing
How shade's for posterity

Confuzione (lesson no. 2)
How attach war image
To simple house repair

"Yeah no, that's it, man
How detach a poetics from
Professional Security Services"

TUB WATER

See, the thing is
Something's gotta click quick
Water's cooling down

Make hay out of
Tub or Water or
Even Hay itself

Hurry man
But no making a Hash
Out of Hurry, either

FLAGGER

Rare sight to see
In the Crescent City
But here it is

Through the palms
Over the fence
Twenty yards to the left

Blue St. Andrew's cross
On crimson background
Studded with white stars

Now, as to the fellow
Whose domicile it is
Pics posted openly

How regard that camo onesie?
How respect that AR-15?
How admire that grimace?

Neighbor, as yet unmet
Among hundreds, thousands
Mysteries of days and nights

Still, to *you* we'd say
"Let her loose—let her flap!
On the *front* lawn, huh"

But *that*—is out of range
So *this*—is out of range
Untrustworthy, vanity mainly

RAIN AGAIN

Forty minutes away they say
Front bringing heavy bands
This is a developing story

Couple things I want rinsed clean
Foremost, the English tongue
Followed by doom and the driveway

Thirty-eight minutes away
These grasses know it, or don't
This is a developing story

Couple things I want washed
This ear ringing—incessant
And the din of mammal's suffering

Thirty-two minutes away
Flooding now in Lafayette
Grasses know it there, or not

Where will our sudden streams flow?
How long will our mucky puddles last?
This is a developing story

MEDITATIO SCRIBENDI V

Bertolt Brecht graffiting
An outhouse, edited by
Fanny Howe (you heard it here first)

MS. WATSON

"Ms. Watson loves me!"
What's embossed on the pencil
A sated tiger's face too

What a wonderful thing
Or maybe a wicked thing
Or worse, not *much* of a thing

Must be nice to be loved
By Ms. Watson—who
The fuck—is Ms. Watson?

Let the tiger answer
If it's willing to
Boy—what a grin

ELIXIR BOTTLE

No need to peg what addles the mind to objects
Save for this blue elixir bottle just found

No need to trip on "trans-historicity"
Save for The Big Easy—1890's

No need to annotate, tabulate "inter-causality"
Save for bogus cures to daily ailments

No need to dope the present with "alter-futurities"
Save for a few doodads, hereabouts, thereabouts

FLOATERS

Just *almost*
Took one out

Bike zombies
Just *floating*

Ten per month
Wrong way, yo!

Solid rust
Single gear

Same handles
Longhorn style

Here *he* comes!
Dead ahead

Or worse yet
Round the curb

TA-RA! *screech*
Lucky duck!

Not time yet
To switch tunes

Ok, *now*
Select tune

Take two breaths
Peal away

BLANK PAD

Just lines
Landing on lines
With *whatever*

What comes next
(Guess *this* comes next)
Is what *came* next

But about North Korea
And the Glacier Breaks
And the T-Man and P-Man

Just lines
Incandescent lamps
In deep sea wreckage

Darkness on darkness
A clamorous silence
Freakazoid creatures

No literary trove here
No metaphors, no metonyms
No jingling career trinkets

What comes next?
A fuller pad
Fuller than before

But about Real Talks
And Real Solutions
And Stick-Throwing Apes

The pad is five by ten
With—let's count: fifty pages
Forty-nine blank, *alright*.

MEDITATIO SCRIBENDI VI

Buck naked Martial
Holding a plumed helmet
Chattin' up Lorine Niedecker (how bout *that*)

BIRDS AGAIN

A crow fixin' to crow out
Crashes into cranky same

A sparrow sparrowing along
Forgetting itself merrily

A grackle enforcing an exclusion zone
Pickin' and pokin' at popcorn

An egret regarding nothing
Hurrying from a hurricane

A pelican—ah the pelican!
Stylin' a slick slash on a sloop sail

All these motherfuckers
Rockin' their range, fully

PRUNER

Felco F-2 classic manual pruner
Corona quick cut forged bypass pruner
Radius garden 551522 pruner

And that's not to mention
Fisker's 911-355 5/8's power lever pruner
Jumpin' outta my skin yo's

Asper BP 3180 1 in. forged steel pruner
Okatsuna 10-48.2 6 in. stainless pruner
Bahco Ergo PX-MX carbon-coated pruner

Feel the blades grazing—smooth
Handle contour's—slick
This spring action—mean ass

About to break out into song, peeps!
Black & Decker cordless lithium pruner
Stop—proceed—*stop*—proceed

Meltex 8.5 in. titanium pruner
No no no—no, AAAH
Tech Rock SP99 3/4 in. dual clipper pruner

Come on come on come on come on
NAH, *nah* man
Hell no, *no* way

Bobcat 20 in. pruner
A.R.S. V58XR rotating pruner
KillCore 19T anvil head pruner

Shshsh—(shsh)—SHSH
There, there there there there there
Yeah yeah—*yeah*—OH YEAH!

BEETLES

This desire or compulsion
To turn a beetle rescue
Into an epic saga

Weightier than "the meaning"
Is the technique
For the time being

Cup hand conically
Swish pool water surface
Till the wriggler's netted

Repeat, but slower this time
There it goes
Lift arm from pool

Now, quick, step to edge
Stretch out wrist
Flick open palm

Now 'meaning'—is on all six's
Hobbled, creeping—'away'?
Or 'towards' something?

Repeat, but much, *much* slower
Is meaning origin—or destination?
Oh, there's another beetle

Focus on technique
Is 'meaning' a rescue—or death delayed?
Oh no! There's *another* one!

SOCIALIZE

Getting on
Getting by
That's the way

Also this
Doin' shit
For shit's sake

Doin' squat
For *something*
Is it too

What is it?
Do I know?
Can I know?

No answer
As always
No change there

So back to
Getting on
Getting by

People say
"How's your day?"
How answer?

Doin' squat
For shit's sake
I dunno

Maybe shit
For squat's sake
Sounds better

DEVIL TREE

Drop the wood chopper joe act
Else, lose the touch

Pimp out a tree for poetry
Forget yourself by sundown

Gnarled branches twisting heavenwards
This tree is a *sexpert*, man

Wood chopper joe's need not consult
There's *shedfulls* of folks to fire up

SKEETER

Global controversy over
Whether this skeeter here
Should thrive or cease to be

A serious debate
About this very species
Raging in rare journals

Upsides to 'cease' are numerous
Goodbye to malaria, yellow fever
Dengue, become academic

Downsides—unknown
A chain reaction perhaps
A species to species downfall

This one's one of fifty-four
Merciless terrorizers of
This glorified swamp/city

Feels good to link it to
A quiet global controversy
Raging at the tip of my pinky

WIND AGAIN

High pressure front building
Behind it a depression
Barometer reads something or other

My level of expertise
In the matter, muttering
Wind again, once

Not "blowing" as we say
But more "escaping"
Wind from wind amid wind

Rushing around what stays fixed
Unfixing that which gives sway
Moving it from here to there

My level of expertise
In the matter, muttering
Wind again, twice

And then it "stills", as we say
Though it can't per say
Except in a vacuum, perhaps

My level of expertise
In the matter, muttering
Wind again, thrice

CRAMMED PAD

Trade war with China looming
My front door ringer's on the fritz

Call your senator first thing in the morning
An idea to get something fixed

I just found—just now—*awesome*
A solution to this crooked table

North Korea can't help this drooping hibiscus
Syria knocking at my door—just poetry (for now)

Iraq sitting up all night in some other's bedroom
GFC circuit, reset properly, often works

Damn griddle not supposed to rust like this
Mexico Mexico Mexico—Russia!

You oughtta—or *I* oughtta—or *someone* oughtta
Wait, somebody's answering—for real, "hey"

LIZARD

Lizard hops out of AC turbine
Appears atop garden tool bin
Zips by on balcony ledge

"O woeful, sinful lizard"
We imagine someone saying
Back in the seventeenth century

And now, it's more like
"Hey lil' guy!
Don't go cray cray chasin' tang"

And maybe something like
"Listen here, g-friend
Punch pause on the pop tartin'"

Or try and imagine
A twenty-second century
Style of address

Lizarda, *course correct* Lizardo
Lizardo, *course correct* Lizarda
The rest of y'all just pile the fuck on

JUST CLOUDS

Ten failed attempts
At Just Clouds
This one's—the one?

"Cottony threads of vapor
Wisp apart slowly
Billowing up again"

Uh—alright—why not
"Blobularities blobularizing
Blobularly"

Um, maybe insert
"I need a brain enema!"
No lie *there*

"Blobularities blobularizing
Blobularly"—*yeah*, yeah
That's clouds—and me

MORNING DEW

Can I quietly exit
While dew's in play?
That is the question

The stage is set
400 by 100 miles
This patch of dew

Dappling grasses, windshields
Slow dripping
Dropping from the roof's ledge

Bubbles clinging vertically
Gravity distending their shape
Till the plop plop, plop

This chorus of trillions
Dampening yesterday's pizazz
Voices fading in the bloom

HELLO NEIGHBOR

Was tempted hard
To go with the title
And nothing else

Hello Neighbor
I'm *still* here
As *you* are

A helping hand
Needed, requested
A swift hand given

This sack of concrete
Rained on, rock hard
Dump on the wheelbarrow

That, and Nothing Else
Sounds like a title too
Sure, you too, take care

ANTS

In the beginning, ants
At the end, ants

Linearly swerving
Ceaseless touch n' go's

Zig zags of economy
Zig zags of duties

Carcass gets schlepped
From here to there

Dismembering's at a pace
Portioning's at a ratio

Next generation gestating
About to get hoppin'

Termites swarmin!
Get in! Get in!